AF686777

SALARY CREDITED.

Now What?

A Simple Indian Guide to Saving, Investing,

Avoiding Mistakes & Building Wealth from Your Very First Salary

The only money book your college never gave you

First Edition | © 2026. All rights reserved.

No part of this book may be reproduced without written permission from the author.

Disclaimer: This book is for educational purposes only and does not constitute financial, tax, or investment advice. Please consult a SEBI-registered financial adviser before making investment decisions. Tax rules, government schemes, and platform names mentioned in this book reflect conditions at the time of writing and may change — always verify current regulations before acting. Examples used are simplified for educational purposes and may not reflect future market performance.

For every first-generation earner in India

who figured out life on their own.

Table of Contents

Introduction

The SMS That Changes Everything

> *"Salary credited: Rs.32,450. Available balance: Rs.32,450."*

You read it three times.

You screenshot it. You send it to your mother. Your hands feel a little shaky.

This is it. Your first salary. The moment you have been working towards for years of studying, late nights, nervous interviews, and anxious waiting.

And now — you have no idea what to do next.

That is exactly why this book exists.

Not because you are not smart. You are. You cracked the syllabus, you got the job, you showed up. But nobody — not your school, not your college, not your company's HR — sat you down and said: "Here is what you do with money when it arrives."

This book is that conversation. The one you deserved years ago.

It is written for you — the IT fresher in Bengaluru paying rent for the first time, the government employee in Lucknow sending money home, the freelancer in Mumbai counting client payments, the woman starting her career after years of preparation, the startup joiner in Hyderabad navigating a new city and a new life.

We will not use complicated jargon. We will not make you feel stupid. We will use real Indian numbers, real Indian situations, and give you a real plan.

By the end of this book, you will know exactly what to do with every rupee that enters your account.

Let us begin.

PART 1

The Moment Everything Changes

Chapter 1

Salary Credited

Ramesh is 23. He just got his first paycheck — Rs.28,000 after deductions — at a mid-size IT company in Bengaluru. The moment he saw the notification, he called his mother in Madurai. She cried. He almost did too.

That evening, his friends dragged him to a restaurant. "Your treat, yaar — you're earning now!" He spent Rs.3,500 on dinner.

The next day, he saw a phone he had always wanted — EMI of Rs.4,200 a month. "I can afford this now," he thought.

Within a week of his first salary, Rs.12,000 was gone. Does this sound familiar?

Freedom vs Responsibility

Your first salary does two things at the same time: it gives you freedom and places responsibility on your shoulders. Most young earners only feel the freedom.

The freedom to buy. The freedom to travel. The freedom to stop asking your parents for money.

But here is what nobody tells you: the rupee you earn today has the power to grow significantly over thirty years — if you treat it right. Or it can vanish into EMIs, subscriptions, and restaurant bills — if you do not.

The financial habits you build early often influence your long-term wealth far more than your starting salary.

The 'I'll Save Later' Trap

The most dangerous phrase in personal finance is: "I'll start saving once I earn more."

It sounds reasonable. It is not.

When you earn more, your lifestyle tends to grow with it. The Rs.5,000 hostel becomes Rs.12,000. The bus becomes a ride-hailing app. The home food becomes on-demand food delivery. This is called lifestyle inflation — and it is the silent thief of your future.

The best time to build your financial habits is right now — when your lifestyle is still simple and a small amount invested regularly can compound into something extraordinary.

KEY TAKEAWAY

The habits you build with Rs.25,000 will protect you when you earn Rs.2,50,000.

EXERCISE

Take 10 minutes. Write your answers in a notebook.

1. What did you feel when you received your first salary message?

___

2. Your dream life in 10 years — where do you live, what do you own, how do you spend weekends?

___

3. How much of your last salary have you already spent or committed? (Be honest.)

___

KEY TAKEAWAY

Your first financial habit matters more than your first salary amount.

ACTION STEP

Open a separate savings account this week and label it 'Savings'.

Chapter 2

Why Schools Never Taught You Money

Kavya scored 94% in Class 12. She cleared her engineering entrance. She got placed in an MNC in Chennai with a package of Rs.6.2 LPA. By every traditional measure, she was a success.

But on the first day she had to file her own taxes, she panicked. She had never heard of Form 16. She thought a mutual fund was the same as a bank FD.

This is not Kavya's fault. It is the fault of a system that taught her trigonometry but not interest rates.

Marks vs Money

Our education system is designed to produce employees, not financially independent citizens. It rewards memorisation over financial intelligence. It teaches the periodic table but not the power of compounding.

This is a systemic gap — not a personal failure. Lakhs of brilliant young Indians step into adult life financially blind every year.

The Indian Middle-Class Money Psychology

Most Indian families pass down a specific set of money beliefs through generations:

- "Save in FD. It is safe."
- "ULIPs are the best investment."
- "Renting is wastage of money. Buy a house as soon as possible."
- "The stock market is gambling."
- "A government job is the safest path — private sector is too risky." (Stability is valuable, but no job guarantees financial security without a plan.)

These beliefs come from real experiences — of people who lived through inflation, bank failures, and economic uncertainty. They are not foolish beliefs. They are simply outdated for the world you are entering today.

You need a new money psychology. One that respects the wisdom of the past but embraces the tools of the present.

KEY TAKEAWAY

A good job gets you a salary. Financial education turns that salary into wealth. You need both.

EXERCISE

List 3 money beliefs you grew up hearing at home:

1. ______________________________

2. ______________________________

3. ______________________________

Now ask: Is each belief helping or limiting me today?

KEY TAKEAWAY

Financial education is something you build yourself — no one is coming to teach it to you.

ACTION STEP

Identify one outdated money belief from your upbringing and look it up today.

Chapter 3

The Biggest Money Mistakes in Your 20s

These are not hypothetical. They are the real reasons why people who earn well end up with little saved by age 30.

Mistake 1: Lifestyle Inflation

Every time your salary increases, spending increases equally or more. The Rs.18,000 hostel becomes a Rs.32,000 apartment. The auto becomes a ride-hailing app. The home food becomes a premium food delivery subscription. Before you know it, a Rs.1 lakh salary feels as tight as Rs.25K did.

Mistake 2: EMI Addiction

Easy EMIs feel like magic. "Only Rs.3,499/month" sounds affordable. But four such EMIs and you have committed Rs.14,000 a month — before paying rent or groceries. EMIs are fine for essentials. They are dangerous for wants.

Mistake 3: The Credit Card Minimum Due Trap

Paying only the minimum due while the bank charges 36-42% annual interest on the rest is one of the most expensive mistakes a young earner makes.

Mistake 4: Buying for Status

A flagship smartphone bought on EMI to impress colleagues. Branded sneakers worn twice. A car loan at 24 to "look successful". Status purchases funded by debt destroy wealth before it is even created.

Mistake 5: No Emergency Fund

Life will shock you. A medical emergency. A sudden job loss. A family crisis. Without a financial cushion, you end up taking personal loans at 18-22% interest — paying a penalty for being unprepared.

Mistake 6: Blind Trading / Crypto / F&O

According to SEBI data, approximately 90% of individual F&O traders lose money. Speculation is not investing. Do not confuse the two.

Mistake 7: Depending Only on Salary

One income stream is fragile. Begin thinking early about skills, side income, and investments that can earn money even while you sleep.

KEY TAKEAWAY
Awareness of a mistake is 50% of avoiding it. You now know all seven.

KEY TAKEAWAY

The most expensive mistakes are the ones you keep making without realising.

ACTION STEP

Honestly identify which one or two mistakes you are most at risk of making. Write them down.

PART 2

Building Your Money Foundation

Chapter 4

Your First Financial System

Priya earns Rs.45,000 a month. She has almost nothing saved at the end of each month and cannot explain where the money goes. She is not irresponsible. She just has no system.

A financial system is a set of rules you decide in advance about what happens to every rupee that enters your account. It removes the need for willpower — because the decision is already made.

The 50/30/20 Rule — Adapted for India

- 50% on Needs — rent, groceries, electricity, transport, EMIs for essentials, family support
- 30% on Wants — eating out, streaming, shopping, travel, social expenses
- 20% on Savings and Investments — SIP, emergency fund, insurance, loan prepayment

If you are sending money home, include that in Needs. The key insight: pay yourself first. When your salary arrives, move your savings amount to a separate account before spending anything else.

Sample Salary Splits — The 50/30/20 Rule

Category	Rs.25K Salary	Rs.50K Salary	Rs.1L Salary
Needs (50%)	Rs.12,500	Rs.25,000	Rs.50,000
Wants (30%)	Rs.7,500	Rs.15,000	Rs.30,000
Savings (20%)	Rs.5,000	Rs.10,000	Rs.20,000

AI PROMPT GUIDE

AI Prompt: Enter the following prompt into your AI tool:

"My monthly take-home salary is Rs.[X]. I live in [city], pay Rs.[Y] in rent, and send Rs.[Z] home to family. I have no investments yet. Using the 50/30/20 rule adapted for India,

create a personalised monthly budget for me. List my Needs, Wants, and Savings buckets with specific rupee amounts and 3 practical ways I can reduce spending in my Wants category this month."

EXERCISE

Fill this in for your current salary:

My monthly take-home salary: Rs. ____________________

My Needs (50%): Rs. ____________________

My Wants (30%): Rs. ____________________

My Savings (20%): Rs. ____________________

Three things I will cut from my Wants this month:

1. ____________________ (saves Rs. ____)
2. ____________________ (saves Rs. ____)
3. ____________________ (saves Rs. ____)

KEY TAKEAWAY

A simple system followed consistently beats a perfect plan followed occasionally.

ACTION STEP

Set up a separate bank account labelled 'Savings' and move your 20% there on payday.

Chapter 5

Emergency Fund: Your Real Security

Arjun lost his IT job in March 2023. He had three months of notice period, then nothing. No offer in hand. Rent was Rs.18,000. Monthly expenses around Rs.35,000. He had Rs.12,000 in his account.

He borrowed Rs.1.5 lakhs from friends and family. The money came back over eight months — but the relationship cost was real.

If he had an emergency fund, this would have been a difficult few months, not a crisis.

What Is an Emergency Fund?

It is 3 to 6 months of your total monthly expenses, kept in a safe and liquid account — accessible within 24 hours when life surprises you.

This covers: job loss, medical emergency, family crisis, sudden relocation, urgent home repair.

This does NOT cover: vacations, sale shopping, new gadgets, or anything that merely felt urgent.

How Much Do You Need?

- Stable job, no dependants: 3 months of expenses
- IT, startup, or gig worker: 6 months
- Single income household or dependants at home: 6-12 months

Where to Keep It?

- High-interest savings account — look for accounts offering rates higher than the 3-year average inflation rate (currently around 5-6%), some small finance banks offer 6-7%)

- Liquid Mutual Fund — redeemable within 1 business day, historically around 6-7% returns, and more tax-efficient than FDs for higher earners
- Short-term FD — good rates, slight lock-in; suitable only if your job is very stable

Do NOT keep emergency money in equity funds, crypto, or stocks. The whole point is that it must be there, in full, when you need it.

AI PROMPT GUIDE

AI Prompt: Enter the following prompt into your AI tool:

"My monthly expenses are Rs.[X] — including rent Rs.[Y], groceries Rs.[Z], transport, and family support. I work in [private sector / government / freelance]. I have Rs.[amount] saved currently. How large should my emergency fund be? How many months will it take to build it if I save Rs.[amount] per month? Where exactly in India should I park this money — FD, liquid fund, or savings account — and why?"

KEY TAKEAWAY

Build your emergency fund before any investment. This is the financial foundation everything else sits on.

KEY TAKEAWAY

An emergency fund is not a savings goal. It is the foundation that lets all other goals survive.

ACTION STEP

Calculate your 3-month expense figure and open a dedicated account for it this week.

Chapter 6

Understanding Insurance Before It's Too Late

Sunita's father was 48 when he was diagnosed with a serious heart condition. The surgery cost Rs.6.8 lakhs. The family had no health insurance.

Sunita, 25 at the time, withdrew her entire savings and took a personal loan. She spent three years recovering financially from a medical emergency that was not even hers.

Insurance is not morbid planning. It is the most practical act of love for yourself and your family.

The Two Types You Need

1. Health Insurance

Even if your company provides group health insurance, get a personal policy. Company insurance disappears the moment you resign — often exactly when you need it most.

- Recommended cover: minimum Rs.10-15 lakhs for someone in their 20s
- Best time to buy: now — premiums are lowest in your 20s
- Including parents on your policy may qualify for a tax deduction under current government tax rules — check the latest regulations each financial year

2. Term Life Insurance

If anyone depends on your income — parents, siblings, spouse, children — you need term insurance. This pays a large sum to your family if you pass away unexpectedly.

- Cover amount: minimum 10-15 times your annual income
- Policy term: until age 60-65, or until your dependants become financially independent — whichever is later
- A Rs.1 crore term plan can cost as little as Rs.8,000-12,000 per year at age 25

WATCH OUT

AVOID THESE COMMON TRAPS

Traditional endowment / money-back policies — these mix insurance with investment poorly.

Returns are typically 4-5% over decades. You do not need to mix insurance and investments.

Buy pure term insurance for protection and invest separately for growth.

ULIPs (Unit Linked Insurance Plans) — high internal charges reduce your actual returns significantly.

Again: keep insurance and investments separate.

Any 'guaranteed return' plan from a relative or agent — check the actual numbers carefully.

If the math sounds too good, it usually is.

AI PROMPT GUIDE

AI Prompt: Enter the following prompt into your AI tool.:

"I am [age] years old, earning Rs.[X] per year, and I financially support [number] family members. I currently have [no insurance / only employer health cover]. Help me figure out: (1) how much term life insurance cover I need and why, (2) how much health insurance is appropriate for my family, and (3) whether I need any other insurance right now. Recommend the

type of plan to look for — not a brand — and what to avoid (ULIPs, endowment plans, etc.)."

KEY TAKEAWAY

The right insurance is invisible when life is fine and priceless when it is not.

ACTION STEP

Get a health insurance quote this week and compare at least two options.

Chapter 7

The Magic of Compound Growth

This is the most important chapter in this book. Read it slowly.

Albert Einstein reportedly called compound interest the eighth wonder of the world: "He who understands it, earns it; he who doesn't, pays it."

What Is Compounding?

Compounding means your money earns returns — and then those returns also earn returns. It is interest on interest. Growth on growth. And the longer it runs, the more powerful it becomes.

> *Rs.5,000 per month at 12% annual returns over 38 years = Rs.3.24 Crore. You invested only Rs.22.8 Lakhs. Time created the rest.*

The Most Powerful Illustration in Finance

Power of Starting Early: Arjun vs Priya

	Arjun (age 22)	Priya (age 32)	Difference
Monthly SIP	Rs.5,000	Rs.15,000	Priya invests 3x more
Years invested	38 years	28 years	Arjun starts 10 yrs earlier
Total invested	Rs.22.8 Lakhs	Rs.50.4 Lakhs	Priya puts in more cash
Wealth at 60 (approx. 12% p.a.)	**Rs.3.24 Crore**	**Rs.1.89 Crore**	**Arjun wins by Rs.1.35 Cr**

Arjun invests less money every month but starts 10 years earlier. He ends up significantly wealthier — not because of luck, but because of time.

The variable that matters most is not how much you invest. It is when you start.

SIP Growth at a Glance

SIP Growth at Approx. 12% Annual Returns

(Illustrative only – actual returns vary based on market conditions)

Monthly SIP	After 10 Years	After 20 Years	After 30 Years
Rs.2,000	Rs.4.6L	Rs.15L	Rs.70L
Rs.5,000	Rs.11.6L	Rs.37.5L	Rs.1.76 Cr
Rs.10,000	Rs.23.2L	Rs.75L	Rs.3.53 Cr
Rs.15,000	Rs.34.8L	Rs.1.12 Cr	Rs.5.3 Cr
Rs.25,000	Rs.58L	Rs.1.87 Cr	Rs.8.83 Cr

What Is SIP?

SIP – Systematic Investment Plan – is a way to invest a fixed amount every month into a mutual fund, automatically. Like an EMI, but one that builds wealth instead of debt.

- You can start with as little as Rs.500 per month
- The money is auto-debited – no willpower required
- You benefit from rupee cost averaging – buying more units when markets are low

Why Inflation Makes This Urgent

Inflation in Action — How Prices Grow at 6% Per Year

Today's Cost	After 1 Year (6%)	After 5 Years	After 10 Years
Rs.1,000	Rs.1,060	Rs.1,338	Rs.1,791
Rs.10,000	Rs.10,600	Rs.13,382	Rs.17,908
Rs.1 Lakh	Rs.1.06L	Rs.1.34L	Rs.1.79L
Rs.10 Lakh	Rs.10.6L	Rs.13.4L	Rs.17.9L

Inflation erodes purchasing power over time. Your investments must meaningfully beat inflation to build real wealth — not just preserve it.

AI PROMPT GUIDE

🤖 AI Prompt: Enter the following prompt into your AI tool:

"I want to start a monthly SIP of Rs.[X] in an equity mutual fund. Assuming a 12% annual return, show me a year-by-year table of how my wealth grows over 10, 20, and 30 years. Then show me what happens if I increase my SIP by 10% every year (step-up SIP). Finally, explain in simple terms why starting 5 years earlier makes such a dramatic difference — use numbers to show me, not just words."

KEY TAKEAWAY

Time is the most valuable input in wealth creation. Every year you delay starting costs you lakhs in your 50s and 60s.

EXERCISE

Your SIP commitment today:

Amount I will start with: Rs. ____________________

Duration I will invest for: ____________________ years

Use the AI prompt above and enter your numbers.

Write the projected result here: Rs. ____________________

That number is the reason you must start today.

KEY TAKEAWAY

The habit of investing consistently is more powerful than investing large amounts occasionally.

ACTION STEP

Open a direct mutual fund account and set up a SIP — even Rs.500 — this week.

PART 3

Growing from Employee to Wealth Builder

Chapter 8

Understanding Your Salary Slip & Taxes

Nandini received her first salary slip as a PDF. She opened it, saw seventeen line items, closed it, and told herself she would figure it out later.

Two years later, she still was not sure why her take-home was so different from her CTC.

Understanding your salary slip is not optional. It is the starting point of every financial decision you make.

CTC vs In-Hand: The Most Confusing Number in Recruitment

CTC stands for Cost To Company — the total amount a company spends on you annually, including contributions it makes on your behalf like employer PF.

Your in-hand (or net) salary is what actually arrives in your bank account after all deductions.

For most freshers at Rs.5-7 LPA, in-hand salary is roughly 65-75% of CTC.

Sample Salary Slip Decoded — Rs.6 LPA CTC

Line Item	Sample (Rs.6L CTC)	What It Means
CTC (Cost to Company)	Rs.6,00,000 / year	Total company spend on you — NOT your take-home
Basic Salary	Rs.2,40,000	Usually 40% of CTC. PF is calculated on this.
HRA (House Rent Allowance)	Rs.1,20,000	Can claim tax exemption if you pay rent
Special Allowance	Rs.1,50,000	Fully taxable. Paid to meet CTC number.

PF (Employee Contribution)	- Rs.21,600/yr	12% of Basic. Deducted from your salary. Goes to EPF.
PF (Employer Contribution)	Rs.21,600/yr	Also 12% of Basic. Employer pays on top. Included in CTC.
Professional Tax	- Rs.2,400/yr	State-level deduction. Varies by state.
TDS (Tax Deducted at Source)	- varies	Income tax deducted monthly per current tax rules.
In-Hand / Net Salary	**approx. Rs.38,000/month**	**What actually arrives in your bank account.**

Key Deductions Explained Simply

EPF (Employee Provident Fund)

Both you and your employer each contribute 12% of your Basic Salary to your EPF account monthly. Your 12% is deducted from your salary. Your employer's 12% is additional. This money earns interest and forms a retirement corpus.

Gratuity

A statutory benefit paid when you complete 5 or more years with the same company. It is included in CTC but not paid monthly.

Professional Tax

A small state-level tax deducted monthly. The amount varies by state — typically Rs.150-200 per month.

TDS (Tax Deducted at Source)

Your company deducts income tax monthly based on an estimated annual tax calculation. You file your ITR (Income Tax Return) at year end to reconcile this.

Income Tax Basics

India has two tax regimes — Old and New. Under the New Regime for a typical fresher, income up to Rs.7.75 lakhs effectively attracts zero tax after the standard deduction. Speak to your payroll team or a tax professional for your specific situation.

TAX-SAVING OPTIONS (subject to current government rules — verify each year)

EPF, PPF, ELSS Mutual Funds, NSC, 5-year FD, Life Insurance premiums

Current combined limit under relevant sections: Rs.1.5 Lakhs per year

Health insurance premiums — deductible for self and parents (check current limits)

NPS extra contribution — additional deduction over and above the above limit

Note: Tax rules change. Always check the latest regulations before filing.

EXERCISE

Decode your own salary slip this week:

My CTC: Rs. ________________

My Basic Salary: Rs. ________________

My monthly EPF deduction: Rs. ________________

My TDS per month: Rs. ________________

My actual in-hand salary: Rs. ________________

Difference (CTC/12 minus in-hand): Rs. ________________

(Now you know where the 'missing' money actually goes.)

KEY TAKEAWAY

Understanding your salary slip is the first act of financial self-respect.

ACTION STEP

Download your latest salary slip and identify every single line item this week.

Chapter 9

Understanding Indian Investments

When most young Indians think of investing, they picture two extremes: a bank FD or the volatile stock market. The real landscape between those two has far more to offer.

Indian Investment Options at a Glance

Option	Risk	Returns	Best For	Notes
Fixed Deposit (FD)	Very Low	5-7%	Beginner	Emergency fund portion
Recurring Deposit (RD)	Very Low	5-7%	Beginner	Disciplined saving
Public Provident Fund (PPF)	Very Low	~7.1% (tax-free)	Long-term	15-year lock-in
EPF	Very Low	~8.15%	Salaried	Auto from salary
NSE Electronic Gold Receipts (EGR)	Low	Linked to gold price	Hedge	Digital gold, no storage risk
NPS	Low-Medium	8-10%	Retirement	Extra govt tax benefit
Index Fund (Nifty 50)	Medium	10-12% hist.	All levels	Best beginner pick
Equity Mutual Fund	Medium-High	10-15% hist.	Patient investor	5+ year horizon
Gold Coins / ETF / EGR	Low-Medium	Linked to gold	Diversification	5-10% of portfolio max
Direct Stocks	High	Variable	Advanced	After building basics

F&O / Crypto	Very High	Unpredictable	Avoid now	90% of traders lose money

Where Should Beginners Actually Start?

A sensible sequence for a 22-25 year old with no investment background:

Step 1 — Build Emergency Fund (FD or Liquid Mutual Fund)

Step 2 — Buy Health and Term Insurance

Step 3 — Start SIP in a Nifty 50 Index Fund

Step 4 — Contribute to EPF and optionally NPS

Step 5 — Learn more, diversify gradually, stay consistent

Do not try to do everything at once. Do not chase returns. Build the foundation first.

KEY TAKEAWAY

Simple, consistent, and diversified investing beats complex strategies almost every time.

ACTION STEP

Identify which step of the beginner sequence you are currently at.

Chapter 10

Your First Mutual Fund

A mutual fund pools money from thousands of investors and a professional fund manager invests it in stocks, bonds, or other assets. You own units of this pool — as the pool grows, so does your value.

Types Worth Knowing

- Equity funds — invest in company stocks. Higher return potential, needs a 5+ year horizon
- Debt funds — invest in bonds. Lower risk, moderate returns, good for short-term goals
- Index funds — track an index like Nifty 50. Very low cost, no manager risk
- Large cap funds — India's biggest companies. Stable and less volatile
- Small and mid-cap funds — higher growth potential but more up-and-down movement

The Beginners' Best Starting Point: Index Funds

For a first-time investor, a Nifty 50 index fund is an excellent starting point:

- Very low cost — expense ratio often under 0.2%
- Tracks the overall Indian economy — no single manager making risky bets
- Historically delivered around 12% annualised returns over 15+ year periods
- Nothing to monitor or manage constantly

Direct vs Regular Plans

Always invest in DIRECT mutual fund plans, not Regular. Regular plans include a distributor commission of 0.5-1.5% per year. Over 20 years, this difference adds up to lakhs.

Use a direct mutual fund investment platform — one that lets you invest without a distributor middleman — to ensure you get the full benefit of your returns.

AI PROMPT GUIDE

AI Prompt: Enter the following prompt into your AI tool:

"I want to invest Rs.[X] per month in mutual funds and plan to stay invested for [Y] years. Compare the following for me using realistic Indian market return assumptions: (1) Large-cap index fund, (2) Flexi-cap active fund, and (3) Small-cap fund. Show projected returns, risk level, and the real difference between a Direct plan and a Regular plan over my investment horizon. Help me decide which combination suits a beginner who wants to invest and forget."

EXERCISE

Open your first direct mutual fund this week:

Platform I will use: ____________________

Fund I will start with: ____________________ (e.g. Nifty 50 Index Fund)

Monthly SIP amount: Rs. ________________

Auto-debit date: ____ of every month

Folio number once done: ____________________

(Writing this means you actually did it.)

KEY TAKEAWAY

Opening a mutual fund account takes 10 minutes. Waiting costs you years of compounding.

ACTION STEP

Set up your first SIP before the end of this week.

Chapter 11

Credit Cards, Loans & EMI Psychology

Rohit has a credit card limit of Rs.1.5 lakhs. He tells himself he will only use it for emergencies and rewards. By the third month, he is paying only the minimum due.

The bank is delighted. Rohit is now paying 36-42% annual interest on the growing unpaid balance.

Credit Cards: Tool or Trap?

Credit cards are powerful if used correctly — they offer cashback, reward points, and fraud protection. Used carelessly, they are the most expensive debt available to a salaried employee.

The Golden Rule: Pay the FULL outstanding balance every single month, before the due date. Never carry a balance forward.

Good Debt vs Bad Debt

- Good debt: home loan (asset that may appreciate), education loan (increases earning potential)
- Bad debt: personal loan for a vacation, credit card EMI for a gadget, vehicle loan you cannot truly afford

How Rs.5,000 Monthly EMI Steals Your Future

The True Cost of EMIs — Opportunity Cost at 12% over 30 Years

(*Approximate wealth foregone if that EMI amount had been invested in an index fund instead)

Purchase	EMI	Term	Paid	Opp. Cost*	Alternative
Bike loan	Rs.5,000	3 years	Rs.1.8L	Rs.1.76 Crore	Buy second-hand

Consumer goods loan	Rs.3,000	2 years	Rs.72K	Rs.72 Lakh	Wait and save
Flagship smartphone	Rs.4,200	18 months	Rs.75K	Rs.90 Lakh	Buy mid-range, invest rest

> *Every EMI you take is a negotiation with your future self. Make sure the terms are fair.*

WATCH OUT

THE **B**UY **N**OW **P**AY **L**ATER TRAP

Instant credit platforms at checkout feel like free money. They are not.

Missing a payment leads to steep fees and credit score damage.

Use BNPL only for planned purchases you will repay in full within the free window.

Treat it like a credit card – pay in full, every time.

KEY TAKEAWAY

Debt is a tool. The question is whether you are using it – or it is using you.

ACTION STEP

List every current EMI. Calculate the total monthly commitment. Is it under 25% of your income?

Chapter 12

Salary Growth vs Wealth Growth

Anil got promoted every two years. By 32, he was earning Rs.1.8 lakhs a month. He also had Rs.3 lakhs saved, two EMIs running, and no investments.

His college batchmate Meera earned Rs.90K at 32 but had invested consistently for 8 years. She had Rs.28 lakhs in mutual funds, no debt, and was buying her first flat.

Income and wealth are not the same thing. Salary growth without financial discipline creates the illusion of wealth.

Multiple Income Streams — Indian Context

- IT professional: freelance projects, technical writing, courses, open-source consulting
- Designer: templates, UI kits, freelance projects, digital products
- Healthcare professional: telemedicine, health content, professional consultancy
- Government employee: tutoring, coaching, expertise-based content
- Freelancer: productise a skill into a template, a tool, or a short course

You do not need to build a business immediately. Even Rs.5,000-10,000 extra per month, invested consistently, adds significant wealth over a decade.

Salary Hike Allocation Formula

Every time your salary increases, resist the urge to upgrade everything at once. Use this split:

Of Every Salary Hike	Goes Where	Why
50%	Increase your SIP	Let wealth grow faster
20%	Lifestyle upgrade	You deserve to enjoy growth
20%	Short-term goal fund	Trip, course, emergency top-up
10%	Give / support family	Generosity is part of wealth

KEY TAKEAWAY

Your salary pays your bills. Your investments and side income build your wealth. You need both.

KEY TAKEAWAY

A well-invested modest income builds more wealth than a poorly managed high income.

ACTION STEP

Calculate how much of your last salary hike you actually invested versus spent.

PART 4

Life, Family & Freedom

Chapter 13

Money and Relationships

Nobody tells you this when you start earning: money will change some of your relationships. Not because you changed — but because money has a way of surfacing dynamics that were always there.

Lending Money to Friends

The most common regret among young earners is lending money to a friend and not being able to ask for it back without awkwardness.

A useful personal rule: only lend what you can mentally write off. If the money never comes back, you should have been at peace with that before handing it over.

"I don't mix money and friendships" is a complete sentence.

Splitting Bills and the Fairness Question

If you earn more than your friends, constantly picking up the tab becomes an invisible financial drain. Use bill-splitting conventions clearly, establish norms in your friend group, and do not feel guilty about tracking what is fair.

Dating and Money Pressure

Romantic relationships in your 20s come with financial pressure — expensive outings, gifts, and maintaining appearances. The right partner does not require you to damage your finances to prove affection.

Early money conversations — however awkward — prevent far bigger conflicts later.

Marriage and Financial Expectations

For many young Indians, marriage brings a sudden expansion of financial obligations: wedding costs, joint expenses, supporting families, and navigating two different money personalities.

Consider discussing these before committing to a partner:

- Do you have compatible spending and saving habits?
- Joint accounts or individual accounts — or both?
- What are your views on supporting each other's families?
- Do you have similar attitudes towards risk and investing?

These are not unromantic questions. They are the foundation of a partnership that lasts.

Women, Money, and Financial Independence

Meena earned her first salary and felt an instinct to defer financial decisions to her father or future husband. She had been told, implicitly, that money was complicated and that others would handle it.

This pattern is worth consciously breaking.

Financial independence is not about distrust. It is about having options and the ability to take care of yourself regardless of what life brings.

- Maintain your own accounts, investments, and insurance throughout your life
- Plan financially for career breaks — maternity leave, caregiving, or other interruptions
- Build your own credit history, not just a joint one
- Know the full picture of your household finances at all times

KEY TAKEAWAY

Financial independence is not about distrust of others. It is about giving yourself choices.

KEY TAKEAWAY

Money conversations are uncomfortable for about 10 minutes. The consequences of not having them can last years.

ACTION STEP

Have one honest money conversation you have been avoiding — with a friend, partner, or family member.

Chapter 14

Money Conversations With Family

You are 24. You have just started investing Rs.8,000 a month. Your mother calls and says the family needs Rs.50,000 for a cousin's wedding gift. Your father says you should buy gold because prices are rising.

What do you do?

The Reality of Supporting Family

Many first-generation earners are also their family's first financial pillar. This is honourable — and financially complex. Include family support in your budget as a fixed monthly amount, not an unlimited obligation.

How to Have the Conversation

Most parents do not understand SIPs or index funds. Do not argue about instruments. Speak in outcomes:

> *"Amma, I am putting Rs.8,000 aside every month in a savings plan. In 10 years it will be over Rs.18 lakhs. If I stop now, we lose all that growth. I already set aside Rs.5,000 a month for home expenses."*

Frame financial boundaries as responsibility, not refusal.

Comparison Culture

"Sharma ji ke bete ne ek sports car li.(Sharma's son brought a sports car)" Indian family gatherings can feel like financial performance reviews.

Remember: you are not building wealth to impress your relatives. You are building wealth to create **freedom**. Those are very different goals that require very different choices.

For Women Navigating Family Expectations

Maya was earning well, but family conversations kept redirecting her savings toward social obligations. It is worth being clear — and early — that your savings have personal goals attached to them.

Your money, your goals, your timeline. Communicate clearly. Compromise where you genuinely want to. Do not simply comply to avoid discomfort.

KEY TAKEAWAY

Financial clarity with family protects both your relationships and your future.

ACTION STEP

Define your monthly family contribution as a fixed line in your budget — not unlimited, not invisible.

Chapter 15

The Social Media Money Trap

You scroll your feed and see a 26-year-old "trading mentor" showing profits on his phone, a finance influencer recommending a specific crypto, a lifestyle vlogger living in a luxury apartment on a "digital nomad" income.

Some of these are genuine. Most are performances. All of them are designed to make you feel behind — so you buy something.

What Is Actually Happening

The trading mentor earns primarily from selling courses, not from trading. The crypto recommendation may be a paid promotion. The luxury apartment is often rented for the shoot.

Social media is not a financial education platform. It is entertainment wearing financial clothing.

What Good Financial Content Looks Like

- Explains principles, not just products
- Acknowledges risk clearly and honestly
- Does not promise quick or guaranteed returns
- Has credentials you can independently verify
- Does not require you to buy something to act on the advice

Quiet Wealth

The wealthiest people you will meet in life often live modestly. They invest aggressively and spend conservatively. They do not need external validation because they can see the number in their portfolio growing steadily.

This is quiet wealth — more powerful, more peaceful, and more lasting than any lifestyle performance.

KEY TAKEAWAY

The people loudest about their money often have the least of it. Build in silence.

KEY TAKEAWAY

The loudest voice in the room is rarely the most financially wise one.

ACTION STEP

Unfollow three accounts that make you feel financially inadequate or rushed.

Chapter 16

Your 10-Year Wealth Plan

Wealth is not built in months. It is built across decades. But each phase has its own priorities — knowing yours helps you focus.

Wealth Milestones by Age — Your Indian Roadmap

Age	Phase	Key Actions	Target
22-25	Foundation	3-month emergency fund Health + term insurance First SIP (even Rs.1,000/mo) Credit score > 700	Survive surprises with zero debt
25-28	Growth	Emergency fund to 6 months 20-25% income invested PPF / NPS started First salary hike reinvested	First Rs.5 Lakh in investments
28-32	Acceleration	SIP > Rs.15,000/mo Net worth = 2x annual salary Medium-term goals funded Multiple income streams	First Rs.25 Lakh milestone
32-40	Compounding	Debt-free except home loan Portfolio rebalanced annually Retirement corpus growing Financial independence visible	Rs.1 Crore+ investment corpus

AI PROMPT GUIDE

AI Prompt: Enter the following prompt into your AI tool:

"I am [age] years old, earning Rs.[X] per month, with Rs.[Y] in savings so far and no major investments yet. My goal is to be financially independent by age [Z]. Build me a decade-by-decade financial roadmap: what I should have achieved by 30, 35, 40, and 45 — in terms of savings, investments, insurance, and net worth. Use realistic Indian salary growth and market

return assumptions. Tell me the single most important financial action for each decade."

Your First Rs.1 Lakh Roadmap

Before anything else, here is how to reach your first meaningful savings milestone:

Your First Rs.1 Lakh Roadmap

Step	Action	Amount	When
1	Open emergency fund account (FD or liquid fund)	Save Rs.5,000/mo	Month 1 — done today
2	Buy health insurance policy	Rs.700-900/mo premium	Month 1 — this week
3	Start first index fund SIP	As little as Rs.500/mo	Month 1 — set auto-debit
4	Update nominees on all accounts	One-time task	Month 2
5	Check credit score (free — once per year)	Free	Month 2
6	Open PPF account for long-term tax saving	Rs.500 minimum	Month 3
7	Reach Rs.1 Lakh total savings + investments	Combined total	**Month 8-12 at Rs.10K/mo**

EXERCISE

My 3 financial commitments for the next 12 months:

1. By ________________ I will
____

2. By ________________ I will
____

3. By ________________ I will

____

Signed: __________________________________ Date:

____

(A commitment to yourself is the most important contract you will sign.)

KEY TAKEAWAY

You do not need to know every step. You only need to take the next one clearly.

ACTION STEP

Pick your single most important financial goal for the next 3 months and put a number on it.

Chapter 17

A Letter to Your Future Self

Dear You,

You are reading this from somewhere in your future. Maybe five years from now. Maybe ten.

I hope things are quieter. I hope you are not checking your phone every night wondering whether you can afford next month's rent. I hope your parents are healthy and cared for.

You worked for this. You started when it felt small. A SIP of Rs.2,000 a month felt laughable to friends booking weekend trips and upgrading their gadgets. But you held on. You let time do its work.

I want you to remember what it felt like when you first read this book — probably young, probably a little uncertain, definitely figuring things out. That version of you made a quiet decision.

A boring, disciplined, invisible decision to show up for your future self every single month.

That decision was everything.

Now — look at the number in your portfolio. Look at the person you have become. Not just financially, but in the clarity and confidence of someone who moved through life without the anxiety that money troubles bring.

You deserve this. You built this. And you are just getting started.

With belief in you,
— The version of you that started

EXERCISE

Write a letter to your future self right now.

Where do you want to be financially in 10 years?

What do you promise your future self today?

____

____

____

____

____

Date written: ______________

Open and read on: ______________ (set a phone reminder right now)

Bonus 1: The First Salary Checklist

Open a separate savings account for emergency fund	[ ]
Calculate your 50/30/20 split (use the AI prompt in this chapter)	[ ]
Start a SIP — even Rs.500 counts today	[ ]
Buy personal health insurance (independent of employer cover)	[ ]
Buy term life insurance if anyone depends on your income	[ ]
Update nominee details on all accounts and policies	[ ]
Set up auto-debit for SIP on salary credit date (with buffer)	[ ]
Get a free credit score check — one free check per year	[ ]
Open a PPF account for long-term tax-free savings	[ ]
Understand your EPF contributions and check your UAN online	[ ]
Decode your full salary slip (see Chapter 8)	[ ]
Identify and close any bad debt	[ ]

Bonus 2: Financial Terms Explained Simply

Term	Meaning
CAGR	Compound Annual Growth Rate — the yearly growth rate of an investment over multiple years, assuming profits are reinvested.
SIP	Systematic Investment Plan — investing a fixed amount monthly into a mutual fund, automatically.
NAV	Net Asset Value — the per-unit price of a mutual fund. If NAV is Rs.50 and you invest Rs.5,000, you get 100 units.
Inflation	The general rise in prices over time. Rs.100 today buys less than Rs.100 did 10 years ago. Investments must beat inflation.
XIRR	Extended Internal Rate of Return — calculates actual returns on investments made at different times, like SIPs.
ETF	Exchange Traded Fund — like a mutual fund but traded on a stock exchange like a share.
Expense Ratio	Annual fee charged by a mutual fund as a percentage of your investment. Under 0.2% is great; above 1.5% is high.
ELSS	Equity Linked Savings Scheme — a mutual fund with a 3-year lock-in that qualifies for a tax deduction under applicable sections.
Bull Market	A period of rising stock prices and high investor confidence.
Bear Market	A period of falling stock prices, typically 20% or more from recent highs.
EPF	Employee Provident Fund — a retirement savings scheme where you and your employer each contribute 12% of your Basic Salary.
PPF	Public Provident Fund — government-backed scheme with tax-free interest and a 15-year lock-in. Check current interest rates.
NPS	National Pension System — government retirement scheme with additional tax benefits over and above the 80C-equivalent limit.

TDS	Tax Deducted at Source — income tax deducted from your salary monthly by your employer.
CTC	Cost to Company — total employer spend on you annually. Not the same as your take-home salary.
EGR	NSE Electronic Gold Receipt — a digital form of gold traded on the stock exchange. No physical storage or making charges.

Bonus 3: Recommended Platforms & Resources

Note: Always verify current status, reviews, and regulatory standing before using any financial platform. This list reflects conditions at the time of writing.

Platform	Website	What It Offers
RBI Financial Education	financialeducation.rbi.org.in	Free, official financial literacy resources from the Reserve Bank of India. Excellent for basics and consumer rights.
CIBIL / Experian	cibil.com	Check your credit score once a year for free. A good credit score unlocks lower interest rates on future loans.
DigiLocker	digilocker.gov.in	Government-backed digital document locker. Store PAN, Aadhaar, insurance policies, vehicle RC, and more securely.
CAMS (Computer Age Management Services)	camsonline.com	India's largest mutual fund registrar. View and manage all your mutual fund investments in one place — across multiple fund houses.
NSE (National Stock Exchange)	nseindia.com	Official stock exchange of India. Use for real-time market data, NSE EGR (digital gold), and

		learning resources on Indian markets.

Bonus 4: Monthly Budget Template

Print this or copy it into a notes app. Fill it at the start of every month.

Monthly Budget Template — Fill This Each Month

Category	Item	Budget	Actual
NEEDS	Rent / PG	______________	______________
NEEDS	Groceries & kitchen	______________	______________
NEEDS	Transport	______________	______________
NEEDS	Utilities & phone	______________	______________
NEEDS	Family support	______________	______________
NEEDS	Loan EMIs (essential)	______________	______________
WANTS	On-demand food delivery	______________	______________
WANTS	Shopping & clothing	______________	______________
WANTS	Entertainment / streaming	______________	______________
WANTS	Travel	______________	______________
WANTS	Social / gifting	______________	______________
SAVINGS	Emergency fund top-up	______________	______________
SAVINGS	Investment SIP	______________	______________
SAVINGS	Insurance premiums	______________	______________

Total Needs: Rs. __________________ (aim: under 50%)

Total Wants: Rs. __________________ (aim: under 30%)

Total Savings: Rs. __________________ (aim: at least 20%)

Bonus 5: Annual Money Review Worksheet

Do this once a year, ideally every January or on your work anniversary.

EXERCISE

ANNUAL MONEY REVIEW — Do This Every January

1. Total savings + investments today: Rs. ________________

   Same time last year: Rs. ________________

   Growth this year: Rs. ________________

2. Monthly SIP amount today: Rs. ________________

   Did I increase it after my last hike? Yes / No

3. Emergency fund covers ____ months of expenses

4. Insurance policies active: Health [ ] Term [ ] Other ____

5. Biggest financial win this year:

   ____

6. One financial habit I will add next year:

   ____

7. One financial mistake I will not repeat:

   ____

FINANCIAL RED FLAGS — If You Check 3 or More, Act Now

[ ] No emergency fund at all

[ ] More than 2 active EMIs

[ ] Paying only the minimum due on a credit card

[ ] No health insurance beyond employer cover

[ ] No investments after 6+ months of earning

[ ] Borrowing money for daily expenses or lifestyle

[ ] Sending money to trading / crypto without understanding it

[ ] No idea what your credit score is

[ ] Dread checking your bank balance

[ ] All money gone before end of month, every month

All Calculators in One Place

Open any free AI assistant and enter the following prompt into your AI tool. Replace the [bracketed] values with your own numbers.

Ch. 4 — Budget Planner: Ask AI to split your salary using the 50/30/20 rule for India

Ch. 5 — Emergency Fund: Ask AI how large your fund should be and where to park it

Ch. 6 — Insurance: Ask AI how much term and health cover your family needs

Ch. 7 — SIP + Compounding: Ask AI to show a year-by-year SIP growth table with step-up

Ch. 10 — Fund Comparison: Ask AI to compare fund types and the Direct vs Regular plan difference

Ch. 16 — Financial Roadmap: Ask AI to build your decade-by-decade wealth milestones

You have everything you need.

Now go build.

www.ingramcontent.com/pod-product-compliance
Lightning Source LLC
LaVergne TN
LVHW101617210926
848480LV00009B/796